LIGHTNING
BOLT
BOOKS™

How Do Parachutes Work?

Jennifer Boothroyd

Lerner Publications Company
Minneapolis

For Grace, Jack, and Joe

Lerner Publications Company
A division of Lerner Publishing Group, Inc.
241 First Avenue North
Minneapolis, MN 55401 U.S.A.

Website address: www.lernerbooks.com

Library of Congress Cataloging-in-Publication Data

Boothroyd, Jennifer, 1972–
      How do parachutes work? / by Jennifer Boothroyd.
          pages   cm. — (Lightning Bolt Books™ — How Flight Works)
      Includes index.
      ISBN 978–0–7613–8968–2 (lib. bdg. : alk. paper)
      1. Parachutes—Juvenile literature. 2. Parachuting—Juvenile literature. I. Title.
   TL752.5.B66 2013
   629.134'386—dc23   2012020003

Manufactured in the United States of America
1 — DP — 12/31/12

Table of Contents

What Is a Parachute?

A parachute is a special piece of fabric. It slows an object or a person falling through the air.

These skydivers are floating back down to Earth.

Many people skydive for fun. A skydiver is trained to jump from an airplane and use a parachute to land safely.

A parachute has many important parts.

This is a skydiver's pack. It has a parachute inside.

The main part of a parachute is the canopy. It is made from many triangle-shaped pieces of fabric. The pieces are sewn together.

The canopy is made of fabric.

Cells are pockets in the canopy. They fill with air and open the canopy.

The pilot wears a strong harness. Straps attach the harness around the pilot's legs, waist, and shoulders.

These skydivers will wear helmets when they jump.

Thick cords connect the harness to the canopy. These cords are called lines.

The thicker straps closer to the harness are called risers.

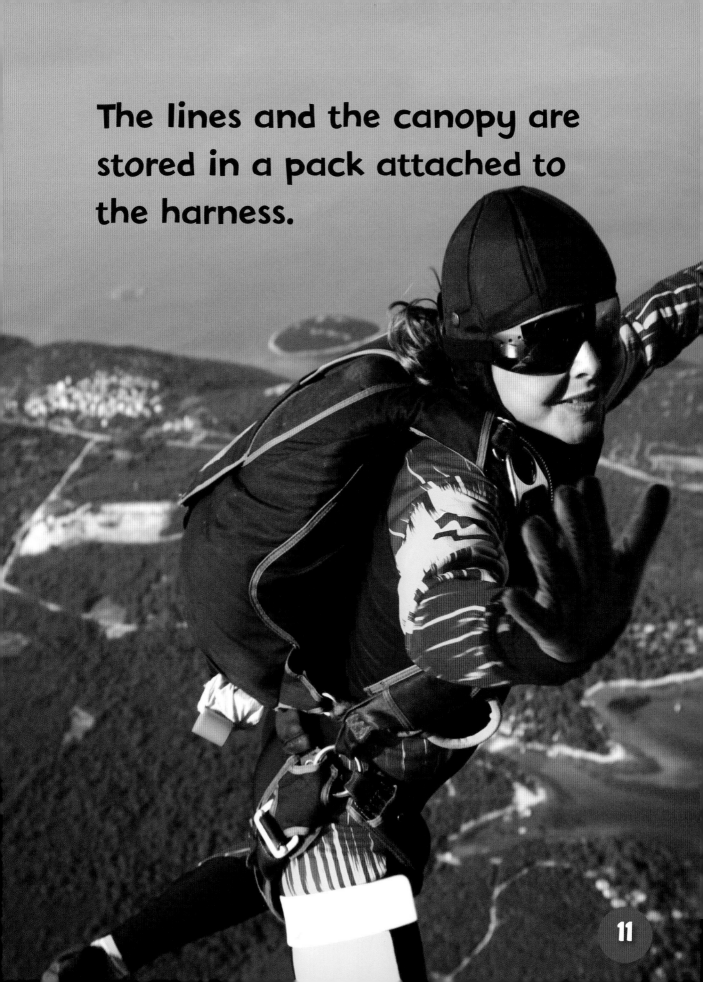

The lines and the canopy are stored in a pack attached to the harness.

Ready, set, Jump!

A skydiver carefully packs her parachute before takeoff.

A parachute must be packed correctly.

The plane flies over
the landing area.
It's time to jump.

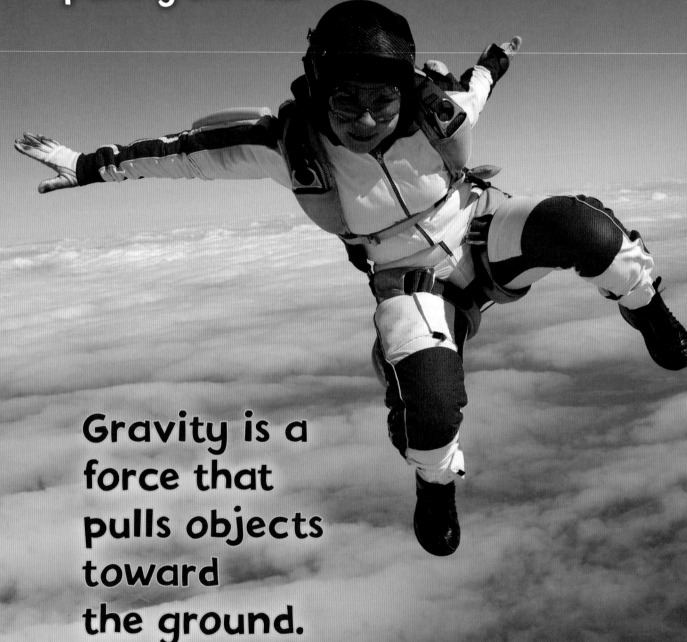

After the skydiver jumps, she falls fast. Gravity is pulling on her.

Gravity is a force that pulls objects toward the ground.

She pulls out a little parachute and throws it into the air. It is connected to the canopy.

A smaller chute slows down pilots when they jump.

The chute is dragged by the air. It pulls open the pack. The open pack lets out the canopy.

The canopy begins to open.

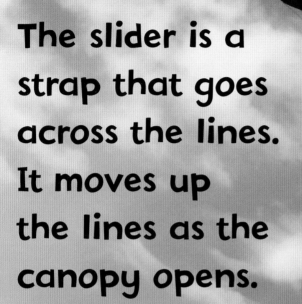

The slider is a strap that goes across the lines. It moves up the lines as the canopy opens.

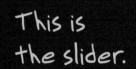

This is the slider.

The slider also makes the canopy open slowly. The pilot can be hurt if it opens too quickly.

The slider keeps the lines from tangling as the canopy opens.

Working against Gravity

Once the canopy is open, the skydiver slows down. The canopy creates drag by catching the air. Drag is the force that slows an object in the air.

A pilot
uses toggles
to steer the
parachute. Toggles are
special handles.

The toggles are connected to the brake lines. The brake lines are attached to the canopy.

This pilot is using toggles to steer with both hands.

A pilot pulls down on the right toggle to turn right. To turn left, she pulls the left one.

Skydivers can twist and turn in any direction.

A pilot can make her parachute move in many ways.

Groups of parachutes
can fall together.

24

Back to Earth

When the pilot is close to the ground, she pulls on both her toggles. The parachute slows quickly.

A pilot needs a clear space to land.

The pilot bends his knees
and lands on his feet. The
parachute falls to the ground
behind him.

It takes practice
to land safely.

Parachuting can be an exciting ride.

This woman is learning to skydive by jumping with an instructor.

Parts of a Parachute

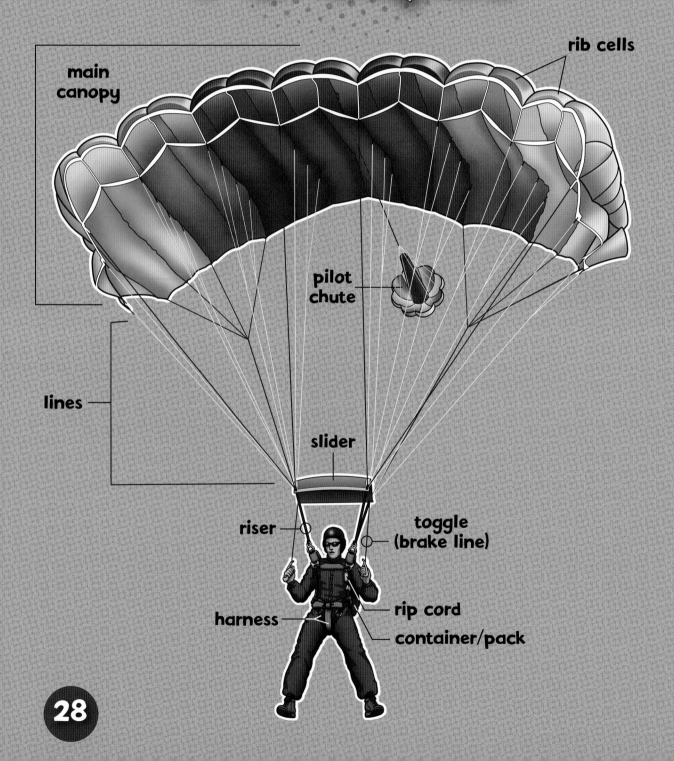

main canopy

rib cells

pilot chute

lines

slider

riser

toggle (brake line)

rip cord

harness

container/pack

Fun Facts

- Skydivers usually jump from a plane about 13,000 feet (4,000 meters) above the ground.

- During a typical jump, the skydiver parachutes to the ground in about five minutes.

- All skydivers carry a reserve chute. This extra chute is used if the main canopy has a problem.

- Skydivers wear a lot of safety equipment such as jumpsuits, goggles, helmets, and gloves.

- During freefall, a skydiver travels about 120 miles (193 kilometers) per hour.

- People must take lessons and complete many successful jumps with an instructor before they have a license to parachute on their own.

Glossary

drag: a force that slows an object moving through air

gravity: a force that pulls objects toward the ground

harness: gear made of straps worn when parachuting

parachute: a device made of fabric that slows an object or a person when falling from a height

pilot: the person in control of the parachute

skydiver: a person trained to jump from an airplane and use a parachute to land safely

Further Reading

Boothroyd, Jennifer. *How Do Hang Gliders Work?* Minneapolis: Lerner Publications, 2013.

Gigliotti, Jim. *Skydiving.* Mankato, MN: Child's World, 2011.

Make a Parachute
http://www.kbears.com/sciences/science-fair/sfparachute.htm

McFee, Shane. *Sky Diving.* New York: PowerKids Press, 2008.

Newton's Apple: Parachutes
http://www.newtonsapple.tv/video_only.php?id=3081

Young, Jeff C. *Pulling the Rip Cord: Skydiving.* Edina, MN: Abdo, 2011.

Index

Photo Acknowledgments

The images in this book are used with the permission of: © Giovanni Mereghetti/
Marka/SuperStock, pp. 1, 21; © iStockphoto.com/Hector Mandel, p. 2; © Stanisa
Martinovic/Dreamstime.com, p. 4; © Oliver Furrer/Photographer's Choice/Getty
Images, pp. 5, 14, 27; © Zorandim/Dreamstime.com, p. 6; © Deymos/Shutterstock.com,
p. 7; © iStockphoto.com/Drazen Vukelic, pp. 8, 11, 13, 19, 25, 30; © iStockphoto.com/
Sieto Verver, p. 9; © Photo Yoko Aziz 2/Alamy, p. 10; © Shay Levy/PhotoStock–Israel/
Alamy, p. 12; © Photo Mere Switzerland/Alamy, pp. 15, 16; © Germanskydiver/
Dreamstime.com, p. 17; © Arrows-Fotolia.com, p. 18; © Dreamframer/Dreamstime.com,
pp. 20, 22; © Daniel Boiteau/Dreamstime.com, p. 23; © Steve Fitchett/Photographer's
Choice/Getty Images, p. 24; © F1 Online/SuperStock, pp. 26, 31; © Laura Westlund/
Independent Picture Service, p. 28.

Front cover: © Ivica Peric/Dreamstime.com.

Main body text set in Johann Light 30/36.

WITHDRAWAL